Perspectives and Reflections

Rishi Neeli

BookLeaf Publishing

Presentation by *BookLeaf Publishing*

Web: www.bookleafpub.com

E-mail: info@bookleafpub.com

ISBN: 9789357741095

First edition 2023

*For my Grandmother who gifted me my
first book*

My Dear Grandma!

My Dear Grandma!
How's it like to be in heaven?
I know you're watching over me,
I know you love me.

Here I sit reminiscing
on a brooding train.
Glancing out to the heavens,
loving memories I retain.

I remember your moonlit face
shining bright as you grew old.
I remember your endearing eyes
warming me up in the cold.

I think about your smile,
weathering away all my fright.
I think about our moments in the temple,
about you teaching me to pray and recite.

I miss your delicious cooking,
meatballs, mango pickles, and rice.
I miss having them together,
you feeding me made them more nice.

I long for your bedtime stories,
of Bethaal and the Panchatantra.
I long for our discussions on the
Puranas, Ramayana and Mahabharata.

I recall you gifting me my first book,
the Little Oxford English Dictionary.
You inspire me to pen my first book,
a collection of self-written poetry.

Its been 2433 days and counting,
since our last moment together.
I wish we had more time,
to say our last goodbyes.

My Dear Grandma!
I miss you so much!
Please keep watching over me,
I know you'll always love me.

My Visit to Salarjung Museum

A towering edifice!
Wondrous to behold.
I step on the precipice,
shimmering in gold.

Across opulent walls,
Liveth thee royal vigor.
O ye Kings!
Eternal is thy grandeur!

Aesthetic murals,
complex ivory.
Uncanny miniatures,
No match for rivalry!

Blazing guns,
ornate shields.
Glazing blades,
the warrior yields!

Sound of metal,
gold, bronze and silver.
Glint of Jade,
symbols of timeless power.

Asia's dragons,
Europe's sculpture.
Arabian tapestries,
immaculate culture.

Come and witness,
history's rebirth!
Blooming to evoke,
the explorer's mirth!

Looking back on a road trip

Where do you find peace?
That's in Nature.
Cruising past landscapes,
serenity of prayer.

Around me dance the lush green fields
to the melody of the breeze.
The Sunflower nods in earnest,
to the sun's passionate decrees.

A chilling mist,
at the crack of dawn.
Tingles excitement,
My heart goes on.

The hushed forest,
whispers darkly.
I travel through thickets,
scouting warily.

Atop the high mountains,
spurning all bounds,
gracefully sways,
the sea of clouds.

Enter the mighty falls!
marvelling beauty.
Smell of the Earth,
mystical singularity.

Birds chirp,
trees hum.
Wind whistles,
thunder clouds drum.

A trip like never before!
The Silver Lining -
"You are never alone."

Hardships of UPSC aspirants

Is there an end in sight?!

Countless books waiting to be read,
some unknown, some forlorn.
Countless hours lost,
burning the midnight oil.

Endless volume of ink spent,
in writing our notes and our lives.
Inspired by toppers,
who guide us to our dream and our doom.

The Mountains of Geography,
the Dynasties of History,
the Rates of Economy,
the Articles of Polity.

Void of guidance,
no way out.
Coaching centres to the rescue,
literally with no way out.

Bloodshot eyes,
loss of sleep and appetite.
Mechanical existence,

no room for fight or flight.

Fever gets a cold shoulder,
stench of medical balm.
All the advice given is,
"Stay focused and calm".

Another year done, another attempt gone
So near, yet so far.
The Dream;
still a flagrant con.

In anguish, we cry out:
"Do we really have an end in sight?!"

The Starry Night (Vincent van Gogh)

The night comes alive in swirls and orbs,
made so by Vincent's crafty hand.

Starry, starry night,
esoteric grey and sombre blue.
Baleful clouds whirl and twirl,
above the lands of hoary yew.

Oh Vincent!
How long have you suffered?
Frenetic yin and yang of your personal demons.
Turbulent mind led astray,
lost in the darkness of your soul.
Perhaps to be found again.

Starry, starry night,
moonlight roils the sky.
Burning stars that brightly beam,
the mournful hamlet lingers like a weary dream.

Holland's church spire,
hailing the cords of Earth and dark.
The flame-like cypress,
waving death's runic wand.
The Starry Night! Looking religiously for the
beyond.

Oh Vincent!
The Starry Night is your darkest ordeal.
The world scorned your love,
all hope lost to the wistful haze.
Your turbulent mind has gone astray,
lost in the darkness of your soul.
Never to be found again.

Climate Change

The sun rises at the brink of dawn,
tenebrous night long withdrawn.
The air is graced by azure skies,
its just like another day, devoid of any surprise.

The world wakes oblivious,
to the perils of climate change.
People act so hideous,
unwilling to make a change.

Thawing ice of the summertime Arctic,
unanswered cries of the Polar Bear.
Alarming surge of sea levels,
cities will submerge, beware!

Towers of concrete and felling of trees,
lethal fumes of the factories,
noxious gases of automobiles,
pushing temperatures to extensive degrees.

Toxic pesticides spoil our food,
hapless oceans, reek of plastic and stiff crude.
Tsunamis, floods and an intense cyclone,
our home is now a danger zone.

Gluttonous greed to exploit resources,
availing the myth of cut-rate green energy.
Global fraternity plays the blame game,
lacking much-needed synergy.

The need is to salvage our planet,
from the clutches of extinction.
The call is for a concerted effort,
involving everyone without any distinction.

Complacency finds no room,
in pushing us to our impending doom.
For it is the end of living,
and the beginning of survival.

An Epistle about Humility

Dear Krishna,

I always wonder and ponder.
Why humility is the sign of acumen?
We do the listening,
but get looked at the other way in return.
We assume responsibility,
and have darts pointing at us.
Is this suffering a sign of acumen,
where gratitude meets hostility?
Sometimes I feel that
our milieu is toxic,
and we have to move on.
Remember the ocean is never still,
and life goes on.

From Rishi

Foreign Universities in India: An Irony

An Oxford in India, they say,
I wonder if it has any branches.
Its time to be liberal,
by taking false chances.

A Princeton in India, they say,
I wonder if we have any money.
We should promote it,
by draining the poor's kitty.

Crushing our universities to a pulp,
what a mendacity?
Extricating foreign universities,
why such pugnacity?

Low cost research,
top-notch results.
Like an Ahm Shere,
in far-flung deserts.

The rush of a blind populace,
fazed by delusion.
Ascending the whimsical overseas throne,
abdicated by realisation.

Offshore coattails,
stand a dark myth.
Reviving native pedagogy,
embeds a firm megalith.

How I fell in love with History

I remember it so vividly, when
I felt royal for the first time.
Marching past elegant busts, like
some fabled monarch.
It all began with a temple,
in the Second City of the Nizam.
Home to timeless paladins,
a heritage out-valuing any corundum.

Caressing past hoary granite,
falling back through the contours of time,
I hear the glimmering music of spears,
a thaw on the sculptor's rock.
I fall in trance to holy chants,
to the king's solemn stance.
I glance through the traveller's eye,
full of magic and majestic fey.
That's when History gripped my obsession:
I embark on a ceaseless journey,
with an everlasting impression.

Tenali Ram's wit in a Limerick

There was a man named Tenali Ram
who was challenged to draw a beautiful
diagram.
He used all his wit,
then fell into a pit,
and finally dozed off ignoring all the flimflam.

Summer's Colour Palette

A golden sun emerges from
a boundless sheet of licorice.
And amber rays flip-flop
through delicate veils of silver.

Emerald hummingbirds
dancing around crimson flowers.
Shy honey bees,
bashful of the bemusing Sunflower.

Weary of bland walls and pallid grey floors,
dreaming beneath placid shades of green.
Yearning for crates of plush mangoes,
biting through sumptuous melons of rouge.

The Aegean sky sprinkles
the showers of Baisakhi.
The mellow orchards sway
to the wood-scented breeze.

Night's sable claws
reach out to the butterscotch view.
The sun sinks deep
into the periwinkle hue.

Marmalade sunbeams converge
like fireflies in the shadows.
And silhouettes arrest every shade,
ensnaring all panorama into black jade.

A Dark Void

I lay cold on damp earth,
gazing pensively at the star-studded sky.
Gloomy thoughts in my head,
playing sombre tunes of insomnia.
Painful memories of the past, and
dreadful prospects of the future.
Hiding beneath the facade of happiness,
trapped in my own mind.
Striving to be the perfectionist,
chasing futile ambitions.
Unbearable anxiety,
eating up my insides.
I long for a shoulder to cry on
but everyone's so preoccupied.
I wonder where do I stand.
Everyone has disappeared,
do they even care?

Above me the moon fades away into oblivion,
tainting every glimmer of hope.
Ominous clouds menacingly float,
horning into my wheezing breath.
The ground diffuses past rationality,

consuming me in a dark void.

Heal

It is important, to heal,
to walk away from quixotic expectations,
accepting that no one is here to stay.

Heal, for the world is a twisted place,
disappointments and failure are at its heart,
ready to knock you out cold.

Heal, because life is never stagnant,
change is constant, you will bloom
in a way you never imagined.

Heal, the scars run in too deep,
I know it stings, you grow strong
only when you endure it.

Heal, begin to feel enough
yourself, that's when you can
truly feel the love you receive.

Heal, don't look back,
your life is not
there anymore.

Heal, your energy is valuable,
don't invest it on the negative,
take care who you grant access to.

Heal, stop hurting your loved ones
by projecting your own wounds
on to them, not even accidentally.

Come let's heal together!
Let's bring out the best in us, and
let's make the world, a better place.

Lagaan: Once Upon a Time in India (2001)

O ye Peasants!
When will it rain?
Gloomy eyes,
Qualm of pain.

O Royal Gentlemen!
Yearning for tax
Pity them wretched,
their empty sacks.

O Bhuvan!
Apple of Gauri's eye
"No Lagaan for three years!"
What is your reply?

"Forceps burn their face,
to remove bread off the furnace!"

O dear Elizabeth,
the guiding light!
Teach them cricket,
ease their plight.

O ye Villagers!
Untouchability taints humanity.
Kachra is a winner,
no use of vanity.

A fiery match,
A conspiracy,
A brilliant hat-trick,
A frenzy!

Nothing comes easy,
then there's magic.
A moment of chivalry,
makes any battle classic.

The shot of a lifetime
An unrequited love
That's how victory resonates
Like the power of Bagha's drums!

The Great Indian Kitchen

A dancer of alluring calm,
sylphlike eyes and graceful charm.
Finds her prince,
and ties the Gordian knot.

Sizzling fritters,
pompous orchestra.
Flushed cheeks,
lurking dilemma.

A cordial welcome,
an amiable ambience.
The weather stays calm,
before any violent storm.

Tradition's her prison sentence,
blocking every step.
Progressive slippers,
left at the very doorstep.

Slick of grime,
across a forgotten face.
Menstruation finds,
an utter disgrace.

"Why does everyone advice,
but never listen?"

Her mettle cracks,
woes of bonded labour.
Soothing raindrops,
hesitant teardrops.

Then:

A flash of courage,
a splash of murky water.
She walks out to her freedom,
leaving behind all torture.

A Strike of Limerence

Ultimately, nothing
to say at first. A

vexing distance.
Flares like a supple rose

on a sandalwood chest.
A crimson apple

gleaming to
a youthful sunshine.

Twilight embers,
inviting the ocean

of stars. Luminiscent
of my reverence.

My heart, waltzing
to the melody of

an angelic harp
Something I never felt before!

I pine for you
to look into my eye,

intrusive and
melancholic.

I wanna scream
my feelings out,

my lungs, bound
by the cords of tragedy.

I give you my love,
only to hang

threadbare.

Me, Chess, and Haiku

Why the King stands firm,
and deft in battle, then falls
prone to checkmate?

City Life

Black crows perch silently,
on telephone wires.
Mourning the march of migrants,
nowhere to go, nowhere to live.

Leaving behind the memories of home,
carrying ambitions made of gold.
Everything here is so expensive,
no wonder their dreams caught a mould.

The loud horns of cars,
resonating echo of a powerful gong.
The street vendor sings his pleas,
the tunes of his survival song.

Charred roads of the urban labyrinth,
lined up by concrete hedges.
Desperate lives struggling to find its end,
settling helplessly around its congested edges.

Millions of people coexist,
in the dungeons of solitude.
Life is trapped in a prison called "technology",
serving the sentence of academic hebetude.

Family ties gone for a toss,
time is too short for it all.
Work, work and work,
lost in the hooks of smoke and alcohol.

This realm of glorious malls and bungalows,
is just an illusion of prosperity.
The bulging colonies of slums,
is the sign of true propensity.

All of this finds acceptance,
in assisting a country's progress.
Rapid urbanisation and development are
contradictions,
pulling the lives of masses into complete
distress.

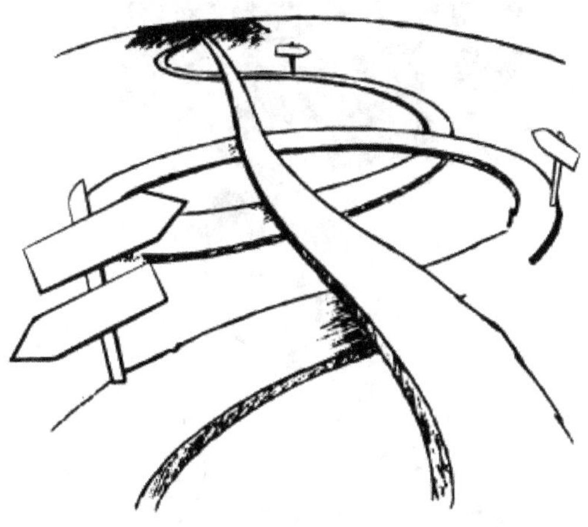

The Cosmos (Acrostic)

The cosmos is an impossibility
Hovering above, a dark veil of mystery
Expanding past infinity

Celestial comets, silver sceptres of the sky
Orbiting planets, divine to the telescopic eye
Shrouded galaxies, imposing gravity outshone
Mysteries of dark-matter still remain unknown
Ominous black holes, humming verses of the
arcane
Strangely Universe, stretching out past the
mundane

Wings of Fire

In this tragic world, its gruesome plight,
the Wings of Fire are burning bright.
Ready to take an inspiring flight,
guided by His Divine Light.

On the serene shores of Rameswaram,
the Wings embark on a glorious odyssey.
From the weight of wartime newspapers,
to the era of complex rocketry.

Reared by Father Solomon,
taught by the cheerful Pandalai.
Spotted by Professor Menon,
groomed by the legendary Sarabhai.

Once distraught to have stopped flying,
driven however by the zeal of always trying.
These Wings of Fire now can't stop soaring,
the wonders of science, always exploring.

Building rockets of brutal strength,
spurring the imagination of every youth.
Guiding missiles of lethal force,
Verve, goal, dedication and truth.

Teaching us how to dream,
the Wings of Fire made a mark.
Longing for a bright future,
three mighty forces set the hallmark.

Desire, strong and blazing hot
Belief, unwavering and resolute
Expectations, realistic and self-driven

The Wings have finally reached the heavens,
leaving us the message of hope and faith.
Kindling little wings to fly high,
The Wings of Fire shine bright in the sky.

Sonnet

What I need now is a poem, well, a fourteen
lines one,
and now a dozen more after this,
to publish a little book on my mind's sea of
obscurity,
then just half-a-dozen more like strings of
pearls.
How freely it goes unless you get
Shakespearean,
and assert the iambic blues must be performed
and place rhymes at the ends of lines,
one for each bend of the track.
But hold on while we chug along the turn,
into the last three where everything will be in
perspective,
where chaos and craving will find an end,
where my heart will tell me to close my device,
release all goofy crude binds,
turn off the lights, and finally hit the deck.